The Simplicity of
Life

Who Are We Really?
Why Do We Exist?

Philip Colagrande

ISBN 978-1-0980-7336-7 (paperback)
ISBN 978-1-0980-7338-1 (digital)

Christian Faith Publishing, Inc.
832 Park Avenue
Meadville, PA 16335
www.christianfaithpublishing.com

Printed in the United States of America

INTRODUCTION

There is so much hate that exists in the world today. Everyone blaming others who don't agree, while searching for the true peace and love we strive for. This book illustrates examples and explanations of what God has revealed to me in my life. I feel compelled to share this with as many people as I can. I pray it gives you the joy and peace that I truly experienced in my life.

There is only one fact and one question that define our life!

Fact: We are all born.

Question: Why?

CHAPTER 1

Questions

Where do we come from?
This question has baffled mankind since the beginning. Scientists, spiritualists, and everyone are searching for the answer, but who really has it? Only when you're nearing death or a tragedy is when we pause. Where am I going? Is this it? Am I going to live again? Or just die!

As we grow and recognize life is ending at some point, why not look for the answers? There's absolutely no control of our time here, and we know for a fact death is coming and yet never search the answer, until the last breath! Our lives are temporal and could end in a blink of an eye. You don't know where you came from or where you're going. So you literally have no real control, do you? There must be a reason.

How We Live

This is an example of what we do here on Earth. You want to acquire a good job that fits your passion. What do you do? Study hard and pass the grades to accomplish this. A plan and purpose. Control. So why (knowing that our life is only temporal) find what the purpose is? Take control. Seek the answer. Why are we here? What should I be doing? I've come to a point in my life that the answer is so simple it's truly ridiculous! I think I've always known, but it's just too simple to be the truth.

Humanity

We all have our wants. Money, beautiful house, nice car, vacations, the very best clothing, good job. We want and want and want. It goes on and on. Of course, that's survival. We're measured by what we have, the lifestyle we live, and for what purpose? *Happiness and joy!* We're proud to accomplish this, and in this world, that's fine. We're so focused on these things that it hides the questions and answers we should be looking for. Answers that really count. If I told you there was an easier way to reach that goal, would you do it? That's the million-dollar question! Always having that joy and peace that we strive for in our everyday lives without struggling to earn it, that's what I found to be true in my life, and to share with people so they could find the simple, simple truth of the real meaning of life!

One phrase: The Lord is my shepherd; I shall not want! What does that really mean? It sounds so stupid! How am I going to live without wants? This phrase doesn't say I shall not need. It says I shall not want! Let's take a good look at our lives. We need food, clothing, a place to live, a car to get from one place to another, and whatever it takes to survive. No question. When you were a child, your parents fed and clothed you, gave treats, went on vacations, had playtime, and everything needed, and you were happy. The reason? Their love, and you knew that. Total trust! Being part of your life was very real! And if you did something bad? They reprimanded you, to teach right from wrong. Sick or down for any reason, they consoled you with their love. If an answer was needed? They led you in the right direction. A love of a parent and child is the greatest love of all! They'll do anything for you, even die! Why? Because you were created by love and made in their image and likeness. You're part of them. Do you notice how you resemble your parents and members of the family? You're created from their seed.

A love without getting love in return is called an agape love. No matter how you treat your parents, or how often you hurt them, they'll always love you. How simple life was when you were a child. Wouldn't it be wonderful as an adult to live that same life? Clothes, food, house, car, everything needed, and on top of that, your playtime, so you can enjoy all the things life has to offer. What a life, no more real struggles. Someone who loves you so much they would do anything for you (*even take their life!*).

I've come to know that I do have a Father who truly loves me like nobody else. The Father who created me to be with him forever. You're saying I'm crazy! That's ridiculous! But is it really? Do you realize without time, you wouldn't exist? There is no time in eternity, because it's eternal. So without time, (you are eternal). Your Father created you and gave life (in time). It could be for twenty, thirty, sixty, or one hundred years, whatever. But it's such a short period compared to eternity. Why? When you die from this time, you'll go there forever. What is our purpose here?

Creation

Have you ever looked up at the stars, moon, and universe? Everything was put just in the right place for this planet to have existence. Over two-thirds of the world is water, yet never consuming the land. Beautiful trees giving oxygen to breathe. Animals, vegetables, and fruits to feed on. The perfect cycle of all creatures that continue to do their job so we're not overpopulated. The amazing sun placed from Earth to have the perfect temperature to survive. Our very own bodies made up of antibodies to fight off sickness and injuries, to heal by itself! *It's amazing!* Have you really thought about this? How do we live? Electricity to warm our homes and light our way; clothing, jewelry, cars, roadways, buildings, bridges, waterways, and all the infrastructures put in place; and steel and manufacturing to make our lives easier. I can go on and on. Everything we use to live was created by us. It just didn't come into existence. It was made by coal, trees for wood, cotton for clothing, etc. So why, after knowing about our very own existence by creating, is it so hard to believe that this world in its perfection was created? Why is that so hard to believe? We have emotions like love, anger, peace, and happiness in our very own souls. Those wonderful feelings of love (came from a rock?) an explosion. Do you realize how ridiculous that sounds? You would need a tremendous amount of faith to believe that one, rather than the simplicity of creation. This is the very reason; we have no excuses! He made it too simple for us to understand.

I'm going to tell you the real reason. It's because of our pride! People don't want to believe that we're mere humans, created by someone, and that our very existence is a gift of life. They can't and will not accept it. When you were born into this world, you came from your parents. You just didn't come into existence. It had nothing to do with you, did it? That's a fact. It was a gift of life. So why were we created? I'm going to answer that with another question. When you get married, why do you want to create children? To make a family to love and take care of the rest of your lives. It's the same with God. You were created to be part of a family and be loved and taken care of for eternity with your heavenly Father. It's that simple. What other reason would he create you? The real question should be, where is he? Why isn't he living with us?

CHAPTER 2

My Story

I'm going to tell you my story and how I came to understand what I believe. Remembering one brief time in my life—just a little boy, four or five—my mother was washing clothes in one of those old wringer machines, and looking up at her, for a second, I thought to myself, who am I? Where did I come from?

Can you believe it? Why would a little youngster think of something like this? It was only a moment. Then I just forgot about it. But recently, I've been thinking, why?

Growing up in my childhood was wonderful. I came from a big family of nine. We did a lot together. My father was a fun guy. Everyone always wanted to be around him, enjoying life to the fullest. My mother was just a saint, always thinking of other people before herself, and so much love in her heart. I felt so warm and secure. Wonderful! As I got older and on my own, I was more like my dad, partying and having a good time. Looking back, I had a great life. Having a strong Catholic background, remembering every Christmas, my mother would write "Happy birthday, Jesus" with canned snow on the mirrors in the house, teaching us the reason for Christmas. I always had a good work ethic. Paper boy at twelve, then later worked for a landscaper and florist. At the age of twenty-four, I started my own business. Everything was just great in my life.

At thirty I opened a second store. The business was expanding, and everything couldn't be better. There were times, I'd go to nightclubs with my best friend and casually talk about things pertaining to the world and God over a beer. That was weird. Why?

This went on for a few months. After a while the business started to take over and I was spending less time out and more time working. I started to change, beginning to see myself yelling at the employees. My demeanor was different, and I didn't like what I was becoming. The happy-go-lucky Phil was turning out to be a miserable, depressed person. I was dating a wonderful woman who loved me very much, and she was seeing the change as well. Then one Sunday night after a wild Saturday, I was flicking through the TV and captured a preacher talking, and as I listened, he caught my attention for a few minutes because what he was saying made some sense. Then I switched to another station and watched a movie. About two weeks later, the same thing happened. Trying to find something to watch on TV, I came across that same preacher, and this time, listened a little longer, maybe ten minutes, then found a movie. After a month, on a Sunday night, being exhausted from a hangover the previous night, again, trying to find something to watch, I came across that same preacher. But this time it was different. Listening, he started talking about things relating to my life, personal, that no one else knew. I had some issues that were bothering me, and he started to say things that had to do with me and those issues. As I intensely listened (he said straight out), there is a man God has been calling for some time now, and said, "You're watching, sitting on a brown couch by yourself." In an instant I got chills and fell to my knees crying like a kid, because I was sitting on that brown couch. He was telling me all the circumstances that were happening in my life that nobody knew. *No one!* I began repeating a prayer, being told that my life was about to change, and God would come and reveal himself. Afterward, I turned the TV off and went to bed.

For the next few weeks, everything seemed to be the same. About a month later, I began seeing things differently. Going out with my friends to the bars and listening to their conversations about women, being vulgar, started to upset me. Telling dirty jokes bothered me. Me, the biggest joke-teller of them all! What was going on? I began noticing on TV seductive women in their advertisements to sell cars, or whatever, and that was bothering me. I didn't know what was going on in my life. Soon I stopped associating with my friends, because I didn't want to be around people that were drunk and vulgar, and I really didn't know why this was happening to me.

Engaged to a wonderful woman at the time, she started to see the drastic change in my life. Why wasn't I going out anymore? Why wouldn't I even have a drink? Telling her it feels wrong and I just don't want to do these things anymore, she thought I was crazy! This continued for a while. One day, in my house, bored to death, I saw an old Bible on the bottom of the lamp table, remembering it was given to me by my mother as a child. Opening the book and going to a random page, I couldn't believe what was happening. It was like I was reading the back of my hand, totally understanding what it was revealing to me, and I couldn't put it down. It was telling me why I was feeling this way and how people would think I'm crazy, not wanting to do the things I used to do, which is exactly what happened to me! As I kept reading, it was revealing what I've been going through for the past few months. At that point, I remembered the prayer that wonderful preacher led me to, asking God to send me his Holy Spirit to show me the way. I told him I was a sinner and asked for his forgiveness and accepted his Son Jesus as my Savior, knowing I meant it while crying like a baby. Continuing to read, it came to a place that told me what being reborn was and how the Holy Spirit enters your body to reveal truths about life and what God sees, and as you start to see through the eyes of God, you start understanding why he's in heaven and we're separated from him. How much he really loves me and why he created us in this world. It told me I would lose interest in what my family and closest friends do. My brother Tom thought I was really off the rocker. We used to do so much together: carousing, drinking, and just having a good time. But when I stopped, he couldn't believe it, because I loved my life, realizing something very powerful happened to me. No other answer.

As a Catholic, growing up I had no interest in the Bible or understood it. Being taught that Jesus died for me and all that stuff really didn't mean anything personal. I was a Catholic, believed Jesus died for me, and if good, was going to heaven. That's it. As I continued to read the Bible, I realized this was a book written for us. A love letter from God telling the creation of life and how to live and why we're separated from him and how much he does love us. The reason I know this wonderful book is the truth? I had an experience in my life that changed everything about me, and then I read it in the Bible. People can't say to me, "You were taught this junk and brainwashed," *so I know this is the truth!* I understand that the Bible is a spiritual book and could only be truly understood and have an undying desire to read when the Holy Spirit literally enters your body. When this happens, God's spirit opens the eyes to your spirit, and it's understood. I never had a desire to read this book or understood it. Why now is it so easy?

How God Speaks

After I came to know God, he started to communicate to me in ways that only I knew and experienced. That's how he talks individually with his children. One time in my life, I felt God left me. (Dry) I can't explain it. Like he was no longer in my life. I needed an answer to an important question. Where does he want me to be? So many people were telling me I should pursue becoming a pastor, and I wasn't sure what to do. Being alone in my mind, I really pursued an answer, asking, where are you, Lord? I started fasting a little to strengthen my spirit while reading the Bible seeking an answer. After a few days, this is how he spoke to me. Amazing! As I was reading, a scripture came to me: John 14:9. It just came to my mind. I went to the passage and couldn't believe what it revealed! Jesus was talking to Philip (my name), and these are the very words he said: "Don't you know me, Philip, even after I have been among you for such a long time?" I broke down after the incredible revelation of God's words speaking right to me. I had so much peace in my heart. My life was never the same after that. The very next day, another incredible thing happened. I read a daily devotional from Oswald Chambers (*My Utmost for His Highest*). Every morning I go to a random page. That morning I opened the book and randomly went to a page 112. The date on top was April 21st, which is my birthday, and the heading was from scripture John 14:9, and in bold lettering it said, "Now Don't Hurt the Lord," and below repeated the scripture and verse ("Have I been so long time with you and yet thou hast not known me, Philip?"). Incredible! It continued to explain the passage. These are the very words from that page.

Our Lord must be repeatedly astonished at us—astonished at how un-simple we are. It is opinions of our own which make us stupid. When we are simple, we are never stupid; we discern all the time. Philip expected the revelation of a tremendous mystery, but not in the one that he knew. The mystery of God is not in what is going to be; it is now. We look for it presently in some cataclysmic event. We have no reluctance in obeying Jesus, but it is probable that we are hurting him by the questions we ask. We look for God to manifest himself to his children. God only manifests himself in his children. Other people see the manifestation; the child of God does not. We want to be conscious of God. We cannot be conscious of our conscience and remain sane. If we are asking God to give us experiences, or if conscience experience is in the road, we hurt the Lord. The very questions we ask hurt Jesus, because they are not the questions of a child. (Let not your heart be troubled.) Then am I hurting Jesus by allowing my heart to be troubled? If I believe the character of Jesus, am I living up to my belief? Am I allowing anything to perturb my heart? Any morbid questions to come in? I have to get to the implicit relationship that takes everything as it comes from him. God never guides presently but always now, and the emancipation is immediate.

If this is not an answer, then nothing is! God will always confirm what he says. What's so unbelievable is that it was explained a third time. I went to church the following Sunday, and the pastor's sermon was the same. In his message he was saying that people always search God's purpose in their life. What should we be doing? And he said God will work through you, no matter where you are or what you do. It's always your choice and not to worry about it. Whether you're a preacher or businessman or laborer, it doesn't matter. *This is how God talks to you!* I was at a place in my life that thought God left me and needed an answer. Wow! Your Father will communicate to you through circumstances that only you and he knows. This is just one of many times God has spoken to me. With all the years of knowing

Jesus and all the trials I've been through, I could write a book on how many times he communicated with me. God is real! You must believe. That's all it takes to know the truth, the hidden mysteries of life.

Trusting God

Continuing to grow in the Lord, I knew that some changes had to be made that were very hard. Going back to that wonderful girl I was engaged to, I kept telling her what she had to do in order to have the same experience in her life. She loved me very much and would pacify, saying she understood, (but to her) just too extreme on some things. This went on for some time, understanding I was standing in her way. Feeling deeply about this, I knew he was telling me to let her go so she could find her own way to him without pleasing me. I was in the way, and it was killing me! I prayed to God and asked him to bring her back, if I let her go, really trusting him. When I broke the engagement, it really depressed me, knowing I was hurting the one who loved me so much, as I loved her, and it tortured me. Days and months passed believing God was working in her life. Then about a year later, I got a call from this wonderful woman telling me she got a job at a clothes store and became close friends to the employer's daughter, who happened to be a Christian. As she continued, I started to tear up, beginning to tell me that she truly understood, and my life reflects what the Bible was revealing to her. I trusted the Lord to bring her back and he did. We were married a year later. I can't begin to tell you what the Lord has done in my life over all these years. We had our first child, a girl, and two wonderful boys after. Three children in four and a half years! (Talk about a change of life!)

As our lives together were growing and becoming more challenging, I started another company with Christmas trees. Two businesses and three children, just five years after we were married. With all the dramatic changes that were going on in our lives, I knew that my wonderful wife was the partner God intended for me. The love and strength she had was unbelievable! A godsend! All the hard work couldn't be matched by her love, strength, and support for me as well as taking care of three wonderful gifts of God just eighteen months apart. I couldn't have had a better loving partner than my beautiful wife.

I always knew my faith in God was real, but as the businesses grew and caring for the family became a full-time job, and then some, I started to spend less time in the Bible, and my relationship with God was slowing down. I felt that my responsibility for my family was very important and my time with God (being less)...well, God would understand. As I continued over the years, I drew further and further away.

CHAPTER 3

How the Lusts of the Flesh Control Our Lives

I had great dreams for the family, working very hard and trying to expand the business, but things just never worked out. Great ideas, but they always fell through and never understood why. God loved me and I loved him, so what's the deal? All the hard work! Why wasn't it paying off? Then a good Christian friend told me he had a dream, and in the dream, I was running around from one place to another and getting nowhere. He asked me how I was doing and what was going on in my life, knowing exactly what God was saying to me, but I just kept at it. Then not too much later, I had a dream. There were two black pouches hanging in the air. Money was coming out of the sky and landing in the pouches, pennies in one bag and fifties in the other. Watching, I realized that the pennies were slowly filling the bag, but when I looked at the other, the fifties were dropping through the bottom because there was a huge hole in it. I knew exactly what my heavenly Father was telling me! "When your mind is focused on making a lot of money without Me in your life, it will never build, because I love you too much to lose you to money. But if you put your trust in Me and do the things that you're supposed to do for the greater good, the little that you make will build and you'll always have enough." (Slow down and smell the roses!)

The Bible tells us Jesus fed five thousand people with just five loaves of bread and two fish. With that little, it was enough to feed the crowd. God has spoken to me in ways like this for many years, and time and time again, I continued to do the best I could on my own, even though I knew he was there for me. I just had to get it done. So I would draw near, then back, near, then back over and over. I just felt it was my responsibility on this earth to get it done. Not going to happen by itself. Continuing on this path, it only grew worse; trying other businesses to help, but to no avail. Venturing out, involving myself in a partnership with Christmas trees and this also failed, then a landscaping business off the tree farm working day and night to provide for my family, again getting nowhere. It wasn't because of doing things wrong; I wanted it too bad, making something for myself, and going to do it no matter what. Many friends and business colleagues couldn't understand why I was struggling so much. They knew the gift that God gave me in sales and saw all the potential contacts over the years and it baffled them. Everything I tried, God would stop. It took years of hitting my hard head on the wall to realize that he would not let me go. He loves me too much to lose me!

One day my wife saw a commercial building for sale and thought it would be a great idea to move my failing floral business to another more prestigious area. Why pay rent when you can own? It was a great location and seemed to be a good idea. I decided to get it. One thing about me, if I want something bad enough, I'll find a way to do it, even if the decision could be wrong. I managed to get the money, only putting me in further debt. Over the years we continued to struggle. It was so bad at one point that my wonderful mother would buy us food to eat for the family. *Can this be?* Can a loving Father let me live this way? All the hard work and effort to make something for myself and be treated like this?

My Way Back

As a child, we think we know everything. Look at your own children. When you begin to realize, we're children to a great and loving Father, who really knows the best for us, then we understand.

God has spoken to me so many times in my life through circumstances and other ways, but I just wouldn't listen. Finally! After all these years of struggling, *I gave up*! That was it. I wanted God and nothing else in this world. To come back, not seeking to see what he would give to help me, because I didn't care anymore about the things in this world, only him, and totally surrendered my life, praying daily, wanting to know him personally as a son should love and know his Father. I didn't care about losing the business or anything. As I read the Bible continually every day, fasting a little so I can concentrate on him spiritually, he started to show signs of his love.

While listening to a radio station, the preacher was talking about taking a person to a new stage in his life, knowing that message was for me. The very next Sunday in church it was the same message. I knew God was starting to work. Then came messages pertaining to obedience. If I felt in my heart that I was doing something wrong, it was time to stop! Start living the right way and quit doing the things that are wrong. Growing in my relationship with God, all fears were leaving. No more worries, because I knew he would take care of me. I really got to a point in my life that I felt free! All the anxieties and frustrations were gone. I really didn't care or worry anymore about my financial needs. Getting closer, everything left, and once again my relationship was strong and I trusted him completely.

How God Orchestrates

As the months went on, circumstances started to change. Before my unconditional surrender, I was thinking about putting a restaurant in the building, and from time to time a good floral customer would stop in the store and offer ideas about the restaurant, being in the food industry. I tried to get financing but just couldn't do it. After I found my Father, he started to take care of it. What's so amazing is the way he did it! One thing about God, it's never the way you think it is. *He knows what's best, not you!* It took me a long time to understand that, and the funny part about it? I no longer cared about my finances; he would take care of it. My needs would be met, no matter what!

The most wonderful thing happened. One day, that very same customer stopped in. Her husband had just passed away, and instead of giving me ideas on a restaurant, she suggested buying her pizza shop. This totally threw me off! Me? Pizza shop? I never expected to hear this, but because of her age and not being able to handle it anymore, she wanted to sell it to somebody that made her feel comfortable and keep it a success. I felt honored, telling her I'd have to pray to the Lord first and ask him if this is something he would want me to do. After saying this, she responded happily, knowing the Lord herself. After receiving the price, I told her I would get back. I prayed and asked, "If it's meant to be, open the door, and if not, close it." Trying to get the finances, the door was shut. I called this wonderful woman and told her I couldn't get it, so it must not be what God wants. (Remember telling you earlier), before my renewed relationship to God, no matter what it took, I would do anything to make it work, and if pursued the same way, probably been in terrible debt, just like before. After a few days, she called me back saying she would finance half of the selling price if I could come up with the other. I couldn't believe what I was hearing. I told her to give me a couple days to see if the doors will open. Once again, not available. I knew God would open the door if it was meant to be. After a few weeks, I called her back and told her how much her offer was appreciated, but it must not be for me. About a month later, this wonderful woman called and told me she really felt I should be the one to own her business and felt compelled, continuing to say if I was able to come up with only ten thousand dollars, she would hold the rest of the financing. Tearing up, I couldn't believe what I was hearing. I felt so much love for her. What a huge heart. This doesn't happen! I told her how much I loved her for such a wonderful offer and would see if I could come up with the money. It's in the Lord's hands. The very next day the money was given to me from a dear friend. I couldn't believe it! Never thinking I would ever own a pizza shop—completely out of my area. I had the worst credit in the world, and this never should have happened. Even after her attorney and family were totally against taking such a high risk, she still did this!

God will orchestrate your life. Not you! He taught me a very important lesson. When you are disobedient, other innocent people suffer. My wife and family suffered only because of me. I knew what God was telling me, but I just wouldn't listen, and it filtered down to my family through no fault of their own. Remember, what you do affects others. This wonderful woman is part of our lives today. God works in unbelievable ways. She still helps with some stages of the business and that keeps her tied to it in some way, which really makes her happy. Her knowledge and guidance have been priceless, and she's part of our family and loved very much (a saint from heaven). The business is very successful, and the thing that goes deeper? If it wasn't, it wouldn't make a difference, because whatever I do, my Father will provide. That confidence can only come from a very personal relationship. Recalling what I said before, as children your parents take care of you, and it's the same with your true Father.

CHAPTER 4

What Real Life Means

Life can be wonderful, if you realize what it means. Let me give you an example. Your life is like a caterpillar. It toils and feeds on whatever to survive, burrowing and working very hard. That's how we live. His real life is a beautiful butterfly, freeing him from this state to become what he was created to be. He doesn't know it. We struggle so much to get what we want and need. It's only for such a short period. Nothing! Think about it. Did you know your great-great-great-grandfather? Do you really care? To you he never existed. His memory is wiped away. That little window of time he lived doesn't exist anymore, and who really cares? All the billions and billions of people that lived don't exist. They're gone. No memory. They could've been the richest or the poorest and it doesn't make a difference. *Who cares!* So what you do here to accomplish your worldly pleasures doesn't matter? Does it? Could there be another reason we were created? This short period is only to see what we can get out of it. That's it? Really? Or were we created for another cause? Why would God, our Father, separate from us? Just ask yourself. Would you leave your son or daughter and let them suffer? No way! What would be the reason for you as a mother or father to leave? There must be a reason.

The Way to God

The people who come to our Lord are only those who need him. Most who have a lot of wealth, life seems so meaningful in their materials. Why look up? But if life is hard, and help and direction is needed, then these are the blessed. When others pray for us, God's power works through our circumstances, as it did for me. My world was material gain, and he allowed me to suffer so I would come home. Jesus again explains this to us in a story he told when he was here. If people would only go to his word and find out what he's trying to tell us. This is the story:

> *Jesus continued: "There was a man who had two sons. The younger one said to his father, 'Father, give me my share of the estate.' So he divided his property between them. Not long after that, the younger son got together all he had, set off for a distant country and there squandered his wealth in wild living. After he had spent everything, there was a severe famine in that whole country, and he began to be in need. So he went and hired himself out to a citizen of that country, who sent him to his fields to feed pigs. He longed to fill his stomach with the pods that the pigs were eating, but no one gave him anything. When he came to his senses, he said, 'How many of my father's hired men have food to spare, and here I am starving to death! I will set out and go back to my father and say to him: Father, I have sinned against heaven and against you. I am no longer worthy to be called your son; make me like one of your hired men.' So he got up and went to his father. But while he was still a long way off, his father saw him and was filled with compassion for him; he ran to his son, threw his arms around him and kissed him. The son said to him, 'Father, I have sinned against heaven and against you. I am no longer worthy to be*

called your son.' But the father said to his servants, 'Quick! Bring the best robe and put it on him. Put a ring on his finger and sandals on his feet. Bring the fattened calf and kill it. Let's have a feast and celebrate. For this son of mine was dead and is alive again; he was lost and is found.' So they began to celebrate. Meanwhile, the older son was in the field. When he came near the house, he heard music and dancing. So he called one of the servants and asked him what was going on. 'Your brother has come,' he replied, 'and your father has killed the fattened calf because he has him back safe and sound.' The older brother became angry and refused to go in. So his father went out and pleaded with him. But he answered his father, 'Look! All these years I've been slaving for you and never disobeyed your orders. Yet you never gave me even a young goat so I could celebrate with my friends. But when this son of yours who has squandered your property with prostitutes comes home, you kill the fattened calf for him!' 'My son,' the father said, 'you are always with me, and everything I have is yours. But we had to celebrate and be glad, because this brother of yours was dead and is alive again; he was lost and is found.'" (Luke 15:11–32 NIV)

If everything is going right for you, there lies the problem. No reason for God! You don't need a God. In your mind your God is your wealth. Your God is your wants. Your God is your things. Your God is your material gain. You need nothing else, but we are missing the true prize. The serenity and peace of a loving Father who will take care of you.

Questions about Sin

Is it something we did and we're getting punished? Why is he in heaven, in another realm of life in the spirit, and we're stuck on Earth? These questions are valid, if you believe there is a God and Father who truly loves you. Look at our own lives. If you have a son or daughter who does something that is terribly evil and wrong, the justice system puts him or her away for life, sometimes death. You probably won't see them again until they've paid for it. Then they're released, right? And this is just, is it not? Well, if we did and continue to do evil, do we deserve to be punished? I know, you're thinking, "What did we ever do that's so bad?" *God hates sin*, not the sinner, so he can't be in our presence, but he wants to. He hates it so much that he died for it by becoming sin in our place. God will judge any man with sin, because all the love he has for us came by his death and agony for you and me on that cross. Only by his death can you be sinless and free from the punishment we deserve and be with him forever. Our fight is ourselves! We make the sin that he hates and are the only ones to blame. Sin will always rule, that's why he made a way. It's like saying, "I blame the drugs that make me this way." Drugs aren't the blame. You are for taking them. If I have a fitting rage and pick up a bat and kill someone, is it the rage or the bat that's to blame? Or is it you?

I have three children. Their first words were "Dada." Do you know what the second word was? *No!* At the very beginning of life, when they start understanding, they're first instinct is to say no and rebel. Without parental guidance and discipline, how do you think they'd turn out? Monsters! Why is it so easy to rebel? At that age, they don't know any better, just doing and saying what feels right. We live in a world (in the flesh) that just feeds its needs, and most of the time, not good. We're just living by our nature, which happens to favor rebellion, and its wants.

CHAPTER 5

Choices

We have free moral choices in our lives. As you grow, your conscience will tell you right from wrong, and you'll know. You can't escape it! So why do we favor choosing the wrong things so many times? We can't help it because we're trapped in these bodies that want to do wrong and then make excuses. We had a chance to be with our Father from the very beginning of creation, but we chose the opposite. He created us to be with him forever in love, and our choice was to know the knowledge of evil. Our natural flesh became evil. God had other plans and tried to save us from this knowledge, because he knew what it did to his angels that fell from grace, because of their evilness. Now, having made our own choices, we face the consequences. I know this seems very grim, but it really isn't. There truly is a reason. God created us to be with him forever in love, joy, and peace without forcing it on us. Our choice, not his. There is good and evil on this earth for a very good reason: to show the difference between the two. He gave us a free moral decision to choose right from wrong. How would you know what good is without knowing evil? He made a creation choosing to know the difference, and it's up to us to decide. Do we want love and goodness or hate envy and evilness for eternity? God made us to have a choice, him or just the opposite of what he is. Do you understand that if we didn't have a choice, God would be nothing more than a tyrant, forcing your love, like puppets on strings, and eventually, wanting the knowledge of evil? So God, with his wonderful grace, let us choose to be with him. Our choice, not his. After seeing what evil does in this world, and being so sick of it, the choice should be obvious. That's what makes the decision you choose so important. Why would anyone want to live in an evil world forever? Thank God for showing us just how wonderful it will be to live with him. He used our choice to turn it into something wonderful. We chose to know the knowledge and we're learning from it.

Why Do We Really Struggle?

What did our wonderful Creator do for us? He gave us a way. From the beginning, evil separated us from him. The punishment is separation. This causes death. God is alive in the spirit and we die in the flesh because he won't live with evil. Once it entered and reigned in our lives, God left. Instead of living in paradise from the beginning for eternity, we chose this death by accepting the knowledge of evil. Do you ever notice? You're about to do something wrong and don't want to, but it's such a struggle, and then you still do it. Why? Because evil is so strong in the flesh.

So now what? Did God leave us? Is he still here? Can we be with him forever? Absolutely! Nobody can really know the answers, unless you read the message given to us, the book written to understand. Your natural body has no interest, because it's hidden in blindness, with the darkness of the flesh. Let me give you an example. If you see a beautiful ruby and that's what you want, but behind it in the rough is a flawless diamond not seen. What if you did? You wouldn't care less about the ruby, and only these special glasses will reveal it. Truth won't be seen unless God opens your eyes through his Holy Spirit.

God's Love and Forgiveness

If you have a son that lived a thousand miles from home, and he was a drug addict and always did terrible things—stealing, lying, cheating, and everything under the sun. You try to help him, but he won't listen. Every so often he'll call you for money to support his habit and that's the only time you hear from him. (What would you do?) Constantly trying to help him, but to no avail. You love him so much, but he just won't listen. Would you send money? If you're a loving Father, the answer should be no. He sees it as not caring and that's all he understands. Now, if the same son had a great job for all the hard work, a loving family who helped people in need, always thinking of others before himself and called you every day, not because he wanted something but because he loves you and wants to know how you're doing, more than likely, you would just send gifts from time to time, because you want to. Your relationship is so strong and loving (common sense). It's exactly with your Father in heaven who created you and loves you like no other! He understands all the struggles we go through and wants to help us, but we refuse to listen. He made a way for us to be with him forever. Remember I told you earlier as a parent, no matter how much your child hurts you, you'll always love him. Even take your own life! That's what God, your Father, did. God's Son, who is part of him, suffered such a terrible and gruesome death for you from his tremendous love. Try to understand what this is saying. There is no greater love than a parent and child. Would you put your child to death for somebody else? Would you?

CHAPTER 6

Justice

God is the judge of the world. Right verses wrong. If somebody does something wrong, they must be punished for it. Let's say you have a loving son and he's murdered. What happens? That person goes in front of a judge, right? He must pay. If that judge just felt sorry and set him free, would that be just? No! The justice system would fail. No matter what that person did, he or she would continually rely on the compassion of the judge. God is a just God. If he did this, you would never be able to take him for his word. There is punishment for evil and sin, period! And what he says must be true, or he'd be a lying judge, and justice would not be served. God, our heavenly Father, knowing that justice must be served in order to have freedom, sent his Son to take that punishment of death for us. Can you imagine seeing your son (who never did anything wrong) suffer a horrible death? And you don't think God loves you? Let me see you do that. After knowing this, some people still refuse to accept his death for freedom and eternal life. If your child suffered and died and you said, "I don't need him for my salvation," what would your reaction be as a judge? I won't even say what I'd do. This message to the world is the greatest love God could ever show, and it must be told. Everlasting life only through his death and no other way. The suffering shows the love he has, and when I hear people say, "God doesn't love me," they truly don't understand just how much! They just don't know it. That's why it must be told.

Let me give you a scenario. A train full of people (that represent the world) and the conductor (representing God), knowing the train is heading for a cliff and the people will die, ties his son on another rail and changes the track just before the cliff and, in turn, kills his son for the world. The worst part? They have no idea just what happened. *No one told them!* That's why God sent his Holy Spirit. To tell the message to everyone through his holy Word and his living spirit in others. If you were on that train and you were headed for disaster, wouldn't you want to know what your Father did for you out of his tremendous love and be compelled to tell others?

Does God Get Angry?

God's anger comes from sin. We're made in the image and likeness of God. Do you have anger? Then why wouldn't he? Evil causes anger with us, so why not with God. We hate what it does to people, and there is justice to rid it from society, and so with God! Common sense. The way you feel when someone does something so awful is the way God feels. Do you think you're above God? Only we can serve justice? The big difference between God's anger and ours is that he loves and shows compassion for the sinner, but not the sin or the punishment. God will forgive the sinner for eternal life, if he accepts the ultimate punishment given to his son Jesus. His anger and punishment will still be for the sinner (just like we feel toward it) if he doesn't accept the punishment taken for him on that cross. It's that simple. The holy word tells us the beginning of wisdom is *fear of the Lord*! Do you realize what he can do, if he really wanted to? You are clay and molded from a Creator. *He gave you life! He gave you love! He died for you!* He made everything! He knows everything about you. The very hairs on your head, your every breath is a gift! The only side he shows is the tremendous love he has for us.

True Answers

God gave us answers in his holy Word. A book that was inspired by the spirit through people that God chose to write this wonderful love letter and message. It explains the creation of the world, why there is suffering and death, how to live the right and peaceful life, explaining everything he did for us since the beginning, time after time since creation, giving us guidance and continually refusing to listen. His patience is beyond comprehension.

I would like to give you another example of our own common lives. How can you know anything unless it was explained? Impossible! For example, if I told a child the house they live in was made by trees and they said to me, "Dad, I don't believe that. How can that beautiful house come from that ugly tree?" So I tell them to read this book and it'll detail illustrations. "No. I don't believe that, and I'm not going to read a book I have no interest in." A few years later, I try to explain the tree and the house again, but this time he listens to me for a little while but still refuses to read about it. After growing a few more years, he opens the book and sees the pictures of the house being built and starts to understand. First the picture shows the tree being cut down then limbs cut and sawed in large sections. Now he notices the bark being removed and he says, "Wow, Dad! I can't believe how different it's starting to look." The next page shows the wood running through a sawmill and coming out in two-by-fours and the frame being constructed. So he says to me, "Dad, this is awesome!" And when the final project is complete, he can't believe his eyes. "How can a beautiful house on that hill come from that ugly dead tree? Now I see, Dad."

What I'm trying to say is that no one really has a desire to read the Bible or has any real interest in it, unless you're guided by the Holy Spirit. That's what opens the word of truth to you. It's a spiritual book and must be guided and seen through the eyes of his spirit. Unfortunately, there are people who pick and choose what they want out of the Bible to fit their lifestyle. Let me explain.

Back to the little boy. Let's say he starts to build his own house from what he saw in the book. And instead of building a strong cement foundation, he decides he doesn't have to do it that way, just leave that part out because it really doesn't matter. He starts off and finishes it. After about a year, a strong wind comes, and the house is destroyed. Now he gets mad and starts to build another—the same way! After a couple of years, the same thing happens. This time he's furious, yelling at his dad, but his dad keeps telling him he must build the foundation first. He still wants to do it his way. It's just like people who choose to listen to parts of the Word of God instead of following the whole truth. They blame God, their Father, for the things that happen in this world without listening to him for the shelter and peace they could have. The foundation is Jesus Christ. He is the only way to the truth for security and peace when the winds of the world (which represent all the problems and anxieties) tumble down on you. The structure you built will not fall, and you'll have safety from the winds inside that home. The tree is cut down first, which means it has to die to this world. The limbs are cut. Then it has to be stripped of the bark, which represents the ugliness of this world. The old self dies. It becomes that beautiful house on the hill. A new creation in Christ. People want to take Jesus out of the equation. They think there has to be other ways to have eternal life. But that is the great lie! To them, people are good, and there are many ways to have God in your life, and sin, as the Bible portrays it—I just can't believe that. According to them, there's good in everything and everyone, even if the Bible says it's wrong. This book was written to those who wanted to know the truth by accepting Jesus in their hearts as their Savior. It's very simple. He chose the humble who have faith to see and understand the truth by his Spirit. And the people who think they know it all? Fools of the world. So please don't make excuses and blame your Father who created you and showed the way, just because you won't listen! If you want the truth, with the joy and peace, then you have to follow the instructions to build your beautiful house on the hill, secured by a solid foundation in Christ Jesus, or it will fall, and you'll blame God for everything, when in actuality, it's you!

Being a Cheerful Giver

God loves a cheerful giver, happy to help others with what blessed you. It's amazing, the power of God, and how he uses others through his great mercy. When God introduces you into his life, your wants are totally gone. These are the people used to help others. If you're not a cheerful giver, then others will not be blessed. Before I came to know God, I wanted everything. I always had to look my best. It was so ridiculous that I didn't even own a jogging outfit. If I was taking out the garbage, I had to make sure my hair was combed and I was looking proper. I wanted the best clothes and biggest house, luxurious car, and whatever I can accumulate. The very first thing that happened to me when his spirit came and changed my life were the wants. They totally left. The Bible verse that says, "The Lord is my shepherd I shall not want," has true meaning. That's how your loving Father blesses the world. It's very simple. If you no longer have the wants, then it's so easy to give back. God blesses you also. He wants you to enjoy the things he gave us in this world, but he knows you won't take advantage. God is awesome!

CHAPTER 7

The Story of Life

Everyone on Earth has a story. The story is about their life and the choices and circumstances that led them to where they are today. I have a story and you have a story. In other words, the *end result*. God and creation also have a story. The real question is, do you want to know it? Or guess and make up your own. It needs to be told to the world.

I truly understand how some people feel, because before all this happened to me, I felt the same way. If I'm a good person and try to live a good life, who are you to tell me I'm wrong? Who are you? I'd be very upset, telling me I'm wrong and you're right. So I do understand. God tells us no one has a right to judge others, and I love him for that, because I'm as much of a sinner as anyone else. He loves me, no matter what I did or still do. This book is not to judge others but an attempt to try to introduce a loving Father into our lives. A Father who understands everything you're going through. He wants (so bad) to help us, if we would just let him.

One day, I was at a restaurant with my wife, and I just started to tear up as we were having lunch. She asked me, "What's wrong?" I began telling her, while sitting there looking at the people. I had an overwhelming feeling of God's love and realized all these people, living their normal lives, had no idea God, our loving Father, was here looking at his children, wanting to hold and hug them, and they had no idea he even existed, or any thoughts about him. I felt that I was seeing through the eyes of God and couldn't stop crying. Could you imagine having a son or daughter that doesn't know you exist? Watching them grow from childhood; seeing them interacting with people; laughing, crying, competing; and they have no idea you're there. Going up to them from time to time, not knowing who you are. All you want to do is hold them in your arms as a caring parent would. This would break your heart. God loves us so much and wants to be part of our lives, the same way with your own child.

Why Don't We Believe?

I've talked to a lot of people over the years who don't believe in God. The biggest reason is anger! How can a caring God let terrible things happen to good people? Why do children die? Why did my family have a terrible accident? Why do people get cancer? The list goes on and on. Understandable.

Remember I told you everything has a story. If you want the answers, you must go to the source, the Creator. He'll give you true knowledge and peace, but it won't be forced. It must be your free choice to believe. Once that happens, then, and only then, will you truly understand better. Don't believe the lie and be trapped by your blindness. You will meet your Father one-on-one when your life ends here, and if he asks you, "Did you ever question your existence? Did you ever seek after the answers when I was calling you through your own circumstances and other people to reveal the truth? Or did you choose to accept your own way?" (Your conscience doesn't lie.) When God reveals himself, it's such a joy, and all you want to do is tell everyone what happened to you. It's so hard.

Let me give an example. You see an angel in front of you and nobody else can. How do you explain it? They don't see it. Our life has a beginning and an end in this world, with a story behind it. How it came to be and why this earth has so much suffering and joy. Don't believe the counterfeit. Example: I have two $20 bills, but one is counterfeit. They look the same, spend the same, but one isn't the real thing, until it's revealed. The lie is exposed. (Another example) If I tell a message to one person and they pass it to two thousand others, each relaying, and one word is left out or replaced each time, it'll be completely different. Those two thousand people represent years on this earth. There is a true story of our life, and it was revealed to us from God, through a love letter he put here thousands of years ago. After all these years, it's been distorted to believe that the Bible is only for the weak, or one book can't be all the truth, other ways, other choices, and what's so ironic? The Bible tells us! Believing the lie! (Amazing.) There are truths that can't be answered or explained unless it's revealed. If a person needs proof, then let me say this. If I asked somebody (after their mom passed away) if they loved her, and they told me yes, and then I said to prove it, you can't. Only you know that, from within. It can't be proven, but you know it's the truth. And if you want to know it from within, then you have to go to the source and let him show you from within.

God has given us a wonderful gift of life with free choices to make. A special time to distinguish between good and evil and our right to choose. He gave us a conscience to tell us right from wrong, so we can't have an excuse. Your Father would never condemn his children without giving them a way to know the difference. It is your sole choice to say yes to be with him and love him or say no. It's in your hands. The few years on this earth is so very short compared to your real life in eternity. You'll either be with him in absolute love forever or without him (with everything he doesn't represent), because you and nobody else made that choice. No one can ever do for you what you can do for yourself.

CHAPTER 8

What Is Prayer?

There's only one thing in this world every single human created can do. You can be blind, rich or poor, black, white, Indian, Asian, deaf, mute, crippled, short, tall—it doesn't matter. Everyone has the power to pray, and it is the single most powerful thing in this world. That's why we are without excuse. Everything we see, he sees. Everything we say, he hears. Everything we think, he knows. Everything we feel, he feels. We think our Creator, our God and Father, is so far away from us in eternity and never realize he's just one breath away. He gave us the most powerful thing in the world: the power of prayer and faith. The reason? To show you who he is. Your faith is proven by the simple fact that you're praying. When he answers, you know he's always with you. Sometimes the answers aren't always what you think they'll be, but he knows what's best. Afterward, you realize he was right. God only wants you to know him as your Father, and the only way to know someone is to communicate. Is there any other way?

When we reach out to people in this world, we talk to each other and develop a relationship that gets stronger and stronger, and as a result, become best friends. And at times when we talk to others and develop love for each other, like your wife or husband, the love is so strong you'll do anything for them. They become part of you. How do you think this all starts? By talking to each other and developing that relationship. It doesn't happen overnight. Trusting and knowing in your heart that you want to share the rest of your life with them. God tells us in scripture we are the bride and Jesus is the groom. That's the purpose of God's love for us. Get to know your Father. He gave us the easiest way. Prayer! Talk to him every day and you'll feel him in your heart and never be the same. He's right here waiting and listening.

Why Does God Not Answer Prayer?

This is how the world thinks. No matter what we ask, it should be answered. Maybe it is. Do you give your children everything they ask for? No. Sometimes they'll ask for things that aren't good for them, but they don't know that. You do! Sometimes no answer is the answer. It could be because it's not time. Or what you're asking will only hurt you. Disobedience? God's here to help, as you would your own children. We don't have all the answers because of our limited knowledge. He's your Father, who truly knows, and you must trust that he understands what's best for you. Always remember, it's the same way you raise your child. Here is just one example: You have your first child, a baby boy, and you're always by his side, feeding, playing, and sleeping with him as a young infant. As he continues to grow, you realize he needs to start sleeping on his own, leaving to break this habit, and he cries out for you. The only thing he acknowledges is that you're not answering and that's all he understands, but you're right outside the door. There are so many reasons why things in life seem so unfair, unsympathetic. We don't see the whole picture as God does. He'll always do what's best for his children, even if we think it's unfair. You must remember that!

When we pray, are we asking God's will for us or our will for us? He always answers, if it's his will for you, because he understands what's best. God's will is for all to be one with him. To have the knowledge of who he is and be filled with the love and peace he has, and not blinded by the things of this world. The truth of who you are and why you were created and how much you're loved. Do you think when you pray for wealth or prestige or anything related to self that it would be answered? Prayer is meant for others to come to the knowledge of who he is. Pray for the wealthy to have a loving and gifting heart to help others who are truly in need, or the blind who don't see God to have their eyes opened. These are the examples of God's answered prayers. We were all born into sin, and for that we die for the punishment. Sin is death. Cause and effect. When we see people suffering from sickness or death, it hurts tremendously! We know this is our life here. This pain that we share is from diseases we created. The chemicals and poisons polluting our land, water, and food for profit gains. Cause and effect. When God created the Earth, it was pure. The age of human life was much longer even though we have to die at some point. When you pray for God to extend his grace to heal those who are suffering and it doesn't happen, the question is, why? God only understands the reason. We will all go through the pain of death, and he will intercede, from time to time, if it's for a higher purpose and plan. That's true faith. Did you ever think that particular person was healed because his life may affect many others in the course of his time here and bring many more into the kingdom? Or the person who was not healed would fall away from God and lose his eternal salvation? God, your Father, knows what's best. Did you ever see the movie *It's a Wonderful Life*? Your choices affect others and changes lives forever.

The Bible tells us a man named Lazarus, a friend of Jesus, was sick and dying. He knew in advance but decided to wait to see him. Jesus was later told that his friend had passed, and he wept! When he traveled to see him, his mother approached and told Jesus he was dead for some time and knew if he was there, Lazarus would've been healed. She had faith, so why wasn't it answered? Why did Jesus delay? *To raise him from the dead!* To show the world that he is the resurrection and life. Anyone who dies from this world and believes will be raised and enter into paradise. Jesus was the first to die and broke the curse of death into eternal life. And those who believe follow. Jesus wept for his friend, but there was a higher purpose. Remember, if God doesn't answer the way you think he should, know for certain he will be raised like Lazarus entering in the kingdom of glory forever, and take peace in knowing you will be with him. That's what we were created for. Jesus taught us how to pray, and these are the very words he spoke:

> Our Father who art in heaven [this tells us God is our Father who is in heaven], hallowed be thy name [holiness, praise, and glory be your name]; thy kingdom come [your kingdom is coming]; thy will be done on earth as it is in heaven [your will be done, not mine on this earth as your will is in heaven]. Give us this day our daily bread [give us today the foods of the spirit as well as the flesh]; and forgive us our trespasses as we forgive those who trespass against us [forgive us for our sins as we forgive those who sin against us—in other words, if I don't forgive others, don't expect God to forgive you, which is very dangerous, because without forgiveness from God…]; and lead us not into temptation [keep us away and guarded by the convictions of the Holy Spirit from temptations], but deliver us from evil [protect us from all evil that surrounds us]. For thine is the kingdom, the power, and the glory, forever and ever [for you are the true kingdom that lives within us and all powerful that no one can deny or come against and all the glory and praise goes to you]. Amen [so be it].

This is what Jesus taught about prayer.

Do Angels Really Exist?

It's a humbling experience to realize the power that exists around us. I've heard stories of others who say angels interceded in their life, but I really never thought about it. God reaches us in different ways, and it's beautiful in the way it transforms our lives. I've always wondered. This is one of my stories.

After coming to know the Lord, there was a time I was in disarray. It was during the Christmas holiday when my business was very busy and hectic. Late in the day on the eve, I left the store to run to the mall to get a gift for my wife. That's me, procrastination at its finest! I was so stressed trying to fit this in on one of my busiest days. When I entered the mall, there was a long corridor before the shops. No other shops were in this space. The length was about one hundred fifty feet. I was about halfway through when a lady approached and asked for change for the phone. (At that time there were phones in the mall.) Without even stopping, just saying as I passed, "Sorry, I can't help you," knowing I did have change but just too rushed. I took five steps. I repeat five steps. Being so convicted, I instantly stopped. When I turned to help this lady, she was gone. Vanished! I became overwhelmed with chills. There's no way she could have exited in that time. Impossible! No other doors were in the corridor. I was astonished and knew that was a servant of God trying to slow me down. I looked up and said to myself to God, "Thank you, for speaking and giving the peace needed," and also saying in a laughing way, "I did stop, Lord," with a smile on my face. I continued in the hallway approaching the stores. There was a large yellow smiley face with flashing lights looking right back at me. Amazing how God speaks!

Intercessory Prayer

If we believe that God is real and lives in a spiritual realm and believe in good and evil because we experience both, then the conclusion is evil and good is in the spiritual. If God is only good, then where does evil come from? We're told in his message; dominions of evil exist in the spiritual. Angels continually fight against the fallen. This is why prayer is so important. It's the most powerful thing you can do for people. When we pray for one another, God sends his ministers of angels to fight against the fallen angels surrounding and manipulating the flesh that we experience. When they battle in your behalf, you begin to see clearly. The strongholds continue to keep you in darkness over shadowing the truth and freedom from yourself.

Legions of angels fight for you. When you stand in prayer for some-one, you're asking the power of God to help in his eternal way. The fight is only spiritual! Nothing you do will ever have a result, trying to force people to believe. Only his spirit and ministers of angels will defeat the enemy and bring the darkness to light.

I get very upset when people say the only thing left to do is to pray. It's the only thing to do! They'll pray for an answer, and when it's met, they make other excuses, and God never gets the praise. For example, if a person is diagnosed with fourth stage cancer and then after praying they get a second diagnosis and it comes back with a different result—nothing fatal—they'll actually say that it was just a wrong diagnosis and the doctors made a mistake. This blows my mind! They completely disavow the answered prayer. Instead of see-ing God's work and changing the results, they'll make another excuse and God never gets the praise! Why even pray? Unbelievable!

The Bible tells a story of a rich man and a beggar named Lazarus. The beggar would ask for crumbs to be given to him off the rich man's table. When they died, Lazarus was in paradise while the rich man was in torment. The rich man asked for Abraham to go back and tell his five brothers what to expect for being evil. He was told they have Moses and all the miracles. The rich man replied, "If I go back from the dead?"

This is how he replied: "If they don't believe Moses, they'll never believe you." In other words, another excuse.

Probably say something like, "you must have been alive and not died." Unbelief is unbelief—period. It's only the power of the spirit that reveals the truth.

What Does God Say about Prayer?

In scripture he tells us, "In everything by prayer and petition, with thanksgiving, make your requests known to God and he will give you a *peace that surpasses all understanding.*" Let's take that sen-tence apart. He is telling us to make your requests to him, and what will he do? Give you a peace that surpasses all understanding. What does that mean? The reason we go to God in the first place is to ask him to answer something that's burdensome, causing you either anxiety, fear, or need. If the burden wasn't there, you wouldn't be making your requests. So how does he answer? *I will give you a peace that surpasses all understanding!* In other words, the prayer is met, because the anxieties, fears, and needs are gone. Others will wonder the calmness through the circumstances you're enduring. Regardless of what's happening, that is the grace of God. When our life is over here and leave to be with our Creator and loving Father, it will be eternal joy. He's giving us a glimpse of what eternal peace is like. No more suffering or needs or wants or fears, but complete peace and wonderful joy forever. It shows our sin nature in the flesh through our wants that cause the sufferings. This has to die to have eternity with him. So the real question is, how do you want to live? Troubles will always be here in this world, but if they have no effect, they don't exist. Peace will reign. Those circumstances will still be there but won't be felt anymore. What a life to know beyond all measures your Father will always provide, always have your back, always love you. Why? Because he created you as a loving child to be with him forever. Why else would he create you?

CHAPTER 9

Why Do We Sin?

What is the greatest force in this world? Water! No matter where you place it, it'll find its way out. The force and power are unbelievable. Water is over 71 percent of the Earth's surface. Your body is made up of over 60 percent. The Bible tells us that what is born of water is water and what is born of the spirit is spirit. The water means and represents the flesh. We can be reborn of the spirit, if we choose to. If flesh represents sin nature, then we need the spirit to fight off the flesh and its desires. Water is a powerful force always trying to find a way out (not to be confined). But the spirit contains it. The flesh has its wants. Get out and go wherever (representing sin). That's why it's so hard to keep under control in our flesh. We're literally a slave to our human desires. When you receive the spirit from God, it sets you free from being enslaved. You start to see through the eyes of God, and his spirit convicts you.

What I experienced (more than anything else) was the love I felt for God and others and the love he has for us. That's what compels you to do good, the love for your Father. Let me give you an illustration; let's say your father left when you were two years old, never knowing him. Your mother tells you not to lie or cheat because it's wrong and it would hurt your father. Would you care about his feelings? No. You don't know him. You never met him, so why care? Now let's say you knew your father all your life and your love for one another was strong, always providing and showing his unconditional love. He catches you in a lie and hurts him terribly. Would you lie to him again? Wouldn't you feel awful, because you hurt your father so bad? If you loved him, absolutely! It's only the love you have for your father that stops you from sinning. The relationship of love is what changes you. You can only feel that love when his spirit enters your body and introduces you to your true Father. The spirit fights off the flesh and contains the water, trying to find a way out. Always! That's why it's so important to stay close to your father and have that personal strong relationship. That power will control you from doing wrong in life.

It's so easy to draw away from God when things of this world start to pile up. We waver and draw back focusing on the anxieties, which is the water trying to get out, but when you draw near to God, the water is trapped. A good example of falling back is like being on a beach and placing your towel on the sand, then heading to the water. You're having fun with the waves, and as you head back to shore, you realize how far you drifted from your towel, not focusing on where you were. That's how simple it could be slipping away from Jesus. Not intentionally. It's just so easy to get involved with the things of this world. It will chock up the real peace and joy. This is the very reason some people dislike Christians. When a Christian does wrong, they think it's all a farce. It's sad, because they don't understand the story. No one is sinless! Let me say this again. Nobody is sinless! Christians fight every day of their lives to stay close to God, which contain the desires of the flesh (water) from trying to get out, and from time to time, the water does get out. We know that we're only saved by the grace and mercy of God. Christians aren't saying they're perfect and special? They are saying. Thank God for his mercy and death that took our punishment. We can never earn our way to eternal life. It's only through the love of Jesus! But because people don't understand, they criticize. Jesus took the punishment of sin for every single person created. No one can earn their way to eternal glory. Example: let's say a certain state represents people in the world that seem to be the best and most righteous. They give to the poor. They seem to be humble, just great people. You can't really say anything bad about them. But these people don't know Jesus and don't want to accept his death for their sins. Now another state represents those that seem to be good from time to time. Just ordinary people who try to do the best they can, but at times they do wrong and even horrible things. But these people are heartfelt sorry for what they've done, asking God for their forgiveness and trying so hard to never do it again. They know Jesus as their Savior, and without him would never have everlasting life. This state represents the family of God. The first doesn't. Who do you think is going to heaven? Obviously, the family of God. Rejecting him now means for eternity. If you've earned your way, then why are you separated from him? God's true family is everyone that accepts his Son of many denominations, not just one, but people who truly believe that Jesus died on that terrible cross for them to have eternal life and a personal relationship. Not all from one religious denomination.

So don't judge others. You're as much of a sinner, separated from God as the biggest murderer. Separation is separation, period. If that murderer gives his life to Christ and accepts that special gift of death on the cross for his punishment, because he repents and asks for forgiveness, God will change him from within and he will be saved, even if his just punishment is served here. If you lie to somebody and tell the world, you don't accept this Jesus to be your Savior because you're a good person, then I pray for you.

Our Lord said he came for the sinners, not the righteous. What he means is simple. If you believe you don't need him because you're righteous, then you'll die in your sins, and only those who know they sin and are not righteous will be saved. He came for those who are humble and realize they need him, not you. If you don't want Jesus now, then why would he accept you after you die? He's giving you a chance and pleading for you to come home. He's your Father and loves you. But is also a fair and just God. The Bible tells us, when Jesus came to this world, he always said, (if a man?) never a command! "If a man comes to me, I will give him rest. If your burdens are heavy, I will make them light. If you knock, the door will be opened. If a man asks for anything, I will give him a peace that surpasses all understanding." He never commands it. It's our free choice. With or without him? If it was forced, would that be fair? No choices in life.

Would that be right? Why live under that control? He loves you too much, knowing the wrong choices in life will keep you apart, and it hurts him tremendously.

CHAPTER 10

Evil and Goodness

I've seen and experienced pain in life just as other people do and have asked the question: why? Most people have. Let me tell you a reference of what good and bad really is. Let's say you have two beautiful children. They're raised the same way, taught right from wrong. Your love is equal. But you noticed one consistently chooses to do bad things while the other good. Why? You brought them up the same way, with all the love you can give. No matter what you do, the one child is just plain bad (trying to take advantage whenever he or she can), no matter who it hurts. You just don't know why. Is it your fault? Absolutely not! Your children were brought up with the same love and respect, but you can't control what they choose to do with their lives. They both have the same free choices to live as they want. One chooses to do evil while the other good. We must face the fact that evil is real, as good is. There will always be the two factors for one simple reason: to know and experience both so you can have an eternal life with your Father (never wanting anything evil in it), because you experienced it. You'll never have to say to your Father, "I want to know what you know, I want to experience both the desire for good and evil." You already did. You chose him and what God stands for, love and goodness. In every aspect of life, you've seen and tasted evil and hate it, never wanting that in your life again. Now God, your heavenly Father, has a creation that chose to live with him from your free choice. Forever! He proved his love for you by doing the unimaginable. He took his Son to suffer an unthinkable, horrifying death, to make a way for you to be with him, to have what you really desire, the life he knows you want and need. Do you remember that butterfly telling the caterpillar what he really is? The free new life he was created to be.

The Greatest Enjoyment

So many people ask these questions: Why do I have to serve a God? Who's he? What's one of the greatest pleasures in this world? *A fine dinner with people that you love and want to be around.* Food is for survival. Without it, you'll wither and die, and it's one of your biggest pleasures. It's exactly the same way with Jesus in your life. We need him to survive, just like the food. He fills us with the greatest pleasure as the fine meal. People think that this Almighty God just wants worship, but it's just the opposite. We literally need him to fulfill our greatest joys we could ever have, a real life to the fullest for which we were created!

Jesus is called *the light of the world!* Look at sun in the sky. It's always there and never leaves from that spot. As the Earth turns away from the sun, darkness appears. When it approaches the sun, there's light. Jesus never leaves. He is the light, but as you turn away from him, darkness will come in your life. When you plant a seed, the sun causes the growth along with the rain. Both. Because the troubles (rain) and the sun being the strength causes you to grow.

CHAPTER 11

Walking by Faith

What does that really mean? When you're an infant learning to walk, your parents will hold your hand. They'll let you go, and you'll fall from time to time, until you learn on your own. It's your desire to want to walk. You must take the initiative. If you want to lose weight, again you must exercise and eat the right foods to accomplish it. No initiative, no weight loss. It doesn't happen naturally. Faith in God is the same. Faith comes by hearing, and hearing comes from the Word of God. You must take the step and be determined to talk to God and develop a close relationship. Your faith will build just like your muscles, but you must want it. As you learn and become close to him, he'll be there to pick you up, just like that child learning to walk. It's a wonderful feeling building a strong relationship with the Father who created everything—your very existence. We have to do things ourselves and he'll be there to help when needed. Our life is based on what we do. The simplest things show how close you are to the Lord and the strength that comes from his spirit through you. For instance, if a friend calls you to help move and you really don't feel like it, but you do it anyway; or someone who wants you to cover a shift at work and you had plans yourself, but realize his plans were far more needy, and you cover for him; or wanting to watch a game on TV but your wife asks you to go shopping with her. These are just some examples that show you must take the step. The result is unbelievable! We have to live in our common place life and do the common place things to show our strength in Christ. Just like the person who exercises and becomes very strong with consistency over time. It's the hustle and bustle in life that glorifies God in you and that only comes from a strong personal relationship, because as you grow in the Lord, it's him doing the work through you. Your determination to seek him out builds that beautiful power that works through you. The power of love! Remember, don't expect God to do miraculous things for you, because he's already doing it.

Who Really Has Faith?

What does it really mean trusting God? There are so many who claim to, but do they really? I always believed, but did I trust him totally? Deep inside, we all know there's a Creator or higher power, and told he's always with us. Do we really believe this, or is it something we just say? *Actions prove faith,* even those of us who proclaim to be Christians. Do our actions prove faith? What actions? Being unafraid, nothing more. Letting go of all your fears, all of them! How can that be? It simply means that you trust your Father to completely protect and take care of everything—finances, health, any problems arising, whatever they may be. We say we believe but still hold on to those fears. The proof that you honestly trust your Father is the action of having no fear, total peace, no matter what.

God illustrates many stories in his word, showing what true peace is using tremendous people in different situations to show us today. Real things that happened in past history written in his word for us to understand. Daniel was put in a terrifying lion's den to be slaughtered because of his faith, and the lions killed others, never putting a paw on him. Why? Because he trusted. Period. He knew no matter what, God would provide.

When Shadrach, Meshach, and Abednego, three men of faith, were thrown into a human furnace because they refused to bow down to the king's image, the soldiers that threw them in were burned to death, getting that close to the fire, but not one hair of these three were singed. The king looked in and saw four shadows walking in the furnace. The circumstances were torture, but they were at peace.

God used these people of faith to show us today what the peace of God truly is.

Joseph was a son from the twelve tribes of Israel who really loved God, and what happened to him? He became a prisoner and slave. He had no idea why God was allowing this to happen. By doing this, he was used to save that part of the world from a great famine that would have killed millions. Although being a slave, the king found favor with him and was treated like a son. God was in control, and Joseph had peace, trusting God.

There are many other stories that show faith, and these people were used for that purpose. You have to let go! Only God will know when you do this, because your fears will show through your actions. Peace is the action. When this happens, you're blessed. You, and only you, will know it. The circumstance will be there, but to you, it doesn't exist. You have to think on these simple terms. If you truly believe there is a Father, who created and loves you more than you do your own children, then why fear? He'll take care of you, just as you would your own children. The difference is, being the Creator of the whole world and in absolute total control, no one else can stand before him! Wow! Give your fears to him and you'll feel the power and peace. This will only happen if you get to know him. Search him. Talk to him. He's right here. Let your heart bring obedience and goodness to your life and God will reveal himself.

CHAPTER 12

What Does Life Mean to You?

If you knew this was your last day, what would you do? Think about it. Would there be fear? Would you go out and party as much as you can? Maybe something you always wanted to do but never had a chance? Bucket lists? What you do defines your life. The actions show what you truly believe. Don't get me wrong; there are people who have peace in their life knowing God as their personal Savior, and doing something special for your life in the end for yourself is fine, but if it's all about you and what you can squeeze out of your remaining time here, it means that you have no other thoughts of the hereafter. No real joy and peace. All about now, self! But if you went out and did something special for someone else and spent your last days helping others, what does that reveal? It shows helping others is far more important and the precious time that we live is more than just about you and what you can get out of it. Your real peace and joy come from knowing it's a testing ground to show what's important to you in life, reflecting the faith to where you're going for eternity. Actions speak paramount! Jesus told us that you are defined in this world by the fruits that we bear. So important. The end-time in your life will show what you believe. Fear or joy and peace! Which would you want?

The Poisons of Life

Your life is a sponge. Whatever your life absorbs fills the sponge, just like liquid. If you put poison in it, then it will absorb it, and that will be the actions of your life. If you fill it with fresh water, it will give life to be shared with others, because you need water for life. It's very important to know what you're filling your life with. That's why direction, guidance, and wisdom are so important. You ever notice the different stories that create the different types of lives? What you're surrounded with, your body absorbs. Your life becomes that, evil or good, God or yourself. So be smart and share your life with those who do good. Stay away from people who poison your life with lies and corruptions. Follow your convictions that the spirit of God is telling you. Your life will be a magnet, drawing those who want the same in their lives. Love, peace, and goodness we all strive. God will work through you, if you let him.

Burdens

Why do we all suffer with burdens? Burdens are nothing more than fears and anxieties. Did you ever hear the saying "I have a monkey on my back"? What does that really mean? Every time something doesn't go our way, fears come into play. Our focus is trying to solve it, which totally disrupts the peace in our lives. We're constantly dragging this fear until it's resolved, which destroys your well-being. It's like having a long chain attached to your leg with a huge boulder at the end. You're dragging it and really can't go anywhere because of the weight, but if someone is behind carrying it, now you have movement and freedom; the boulder is still there but you no longer feel the weight or even know it exists. The boulder isn't gone, but to you, it is. Anxiety is only fear, and if the fear and worry are gone but the situation is still there, you won't feel it, so to you, there is no situation. It doesn't exist in your life. Total peace.

The Bible tells us the apostles were on a boat and a large storm appeared, and they were terrified for their lives. Peter saw someone walking on the water far from the boat, and when he recognized it was Jesus, all he wanted to do was go to him, focusing totally on him and stopped noticing the storm. He walked to Jesus on the water and never realized what he was doing, let alone the storm. Once his eyes and concentration were off him, faith was lost, and his mind on the surroundings came into play and fear entered in, and he began to sink, yelling for Jesus to save him. Jesus reached out and picked him up to safety and said these words: "Peter, why did you take your eyes off me and lose your faith?" The secret to real joy and peace isn't *you* trying to achieve it, because that will never happen. It's only when you rely on no one else, and rely on nothing else, but your faith in knowing beyond all measure that your loving Savior Jesus is there, and he will provide everything you will ever need or want. Remember, the storm was still there (your situation), but Peter never noticed it. That's the will of God for you, believing and being one with him so you can have the life he intended.

The Blindness of Our Lives

What I came to realize is how blind and comfortable I was in the way I lived. It's like being born in a dark cave, and as I grow, the darkness hides everything around me. Then suddenly, noticing a light flickering from a distance, I start to approach, beginning to see my surroundings. First, it was the slimy wet moss around the walls of the cave and the stench. Lizards were all around me. Continuing to approach the light, glowing more, I saw bats eating and fighting with one another, and noticing not far from me, a large bear tearing apart a fawn, and it's beginning to disgust me, realizing all this time I was never being able to see the horrible things surrounding my life, because of the darkness blinding the truth. Continuing, I saw a huge opening with brilliant sunlight exiting the cave. When I reached it, I couldn't believe my eyes! A beautiful blue sky with tremendous and vibrant green trees. A beautiful landscape of lush green grass! All this beauty kept from me because of the darkness in the cave.

We live and do wrong things in our lives because we're so hidden in darkness, and that's all we see. The thing that gives you conviction to do right is the spirit of God, who is the light that flickers. It will show what's in the darkness and what we really don't see. Only your conscience will judge you, and it's up to you, by choice, to accept and see what it exposes. The light is Jesus Christ and the living spirit of God, and it's God's spirit that will judge you and no one else! All the times the light flickered in your life, did you go to see the truth of what it was exposing or did you ignore it and stay in the darkness? The spirit of light is the witness, and you won't be able to escape it. You'll know! It was the truth, but you never accepted it.

Judging Others

Being born into this world is one thing, but circumstances around each individual are different, some around wealth, others poverty. They may have parents together in a strong, loving relationship, while others with one parent or drug-addicted or no parents at all and put in foster care. What God has shown me is how truly blessed I've been. Our divine nature is to help and not judge. That's for God to do, not us! Never think you're better than anyone—for any reason. You have no idea what others have gone through in their lives. But what God did show me is no matter how you came into this world, you're still his child made in his image and likeness. He gives everyone, whether poor or rich, healthy or sick, the same conscience and free choices to make, which will sum up your life—the difference between good and bad. Everyone can see and feel evil and what's wrong, even if it surrounds you more than others. For that fact alone, we should want to have nothing to do with it. Your conscience will always tell you. The surrounding of evil doesn't mean you have to join in. Listen to your heart. God will help and take care of the rest. Trust me! I pity those that define themselves as good people because most of them are the worst. To sum up, you, and only you, are responsible for your life, and only your Creator will judge. We have no idea how God speaks to his child, and only our Father and his child know. Everyone has the light that flickers in the darkness of the cave (this world), and it's up to you to go to it. When it's time to meet your God and Father, it will be one-on-one, no one else there defending, and you'll know without a doubt it was your choice!

CHAPTER 13

Signs

It's amazing how God leaves signs for us to see. When you develop a relationship with your Father, he'll communicate to you in different ways. This is one example: Jesus tells us he is the light of the world; the pathway to heaven; and the Way, the truth, and the life! The next time you travel in your car, you'll see all the wooden poles on the highway. If you notice on top of every pole, there's a shape of a cross. A *cross*! These poles hold the wires for the electricity to light our way. Pole after pole on the roads we travel. When I see this, I see God showing exactly who Christ is and the loving grace and message of our Savior. These poles (to me) show a sign of Calvary, the light to our pathway traveling through this life to heaven and our blessed Savior. It's amazing that two thousand years ago this would be an orchestrated sign for us today. They're everywhere! Without the poles holding the lines that light up our way, we'd be lost and blind. Incredible! The truth is right in front of our face. As I look, I see Gethsemane and the love of Jesus. And it gives me strength every day knowing how much he suffered for me and how much love he has for us all. Let God speak, and look for his signs!

God's Love Right in Front of Us!

When Jesus was among us, he taught that the greatest love is serving others. The least of you will be the greatest! Think about that.

Those that are never recognized are people who are the humblest and show the simplest actions. When you need someone to talk to, they have an open ear. A favor? You know, beyond all doubt, they'll be there. It's the little things in life we take for granted that are the greatest. Those of us who want to be first will be last! The wisest in their opinion are the most ignorant. Amazing!

What I found in this world that shows the greatest example of what true love should be, is in a dog. Your dog is waiting for you every day. If you're having a bad day, mentally or physically, they're right by your side giving you their tremendous love. They'll protect you from harm's way, never complain, and never desert you. Some people abuse these beautiful creations of God, considering them just animals without seeing the true love. Now, look at the spelling of the name. Dog. Backward? God. Complete unconditional love! This wonderful animal of love is always there and a lot of times never recognized, just like God.

Look around and see the beauty of God, the love of your family and friends, the exceptional nature of this Earth made for you—the very existence of the gift of life. God tells us in scriptures, "Be still, and know that I am God." He is only a prayer away, always by your side with open ears and a love beyond measure. Next time you look into your dog's eyes, you are looking into the eyes of Almighty God. A creation by him representing his unconditional love.

CHAPTER 14

Each Soul Precious to God

God created everyone in life with individual personalities. That's what makes each person unique. We all think differently, and he knows exactly how to call you for who you are! Every experience reaches the same result, which is knowing Jesus Christ as your personal Savior and having that wonderful relationship. He also gave different gifts. Example: you have two sons and tell them to get a job and work for a living. One applies right away and eventually hired; the other refuses. He doesn't want to work. After a few months, he notices a car he really wants and asks you for the money. Obviously, the answer is no. After a while his friends ask him to go to a concert, but he can't afford it, so again he comes to you, and the answer is the same. Now realizing if he wants to enjoy life, he has to work for it. In a little while he gets a good job. God approaches us in our lives differently, because he knows us and what we need to approach him. He will use your personality to accomplish the reward. Circumstances in life direct you. The two sons have different jobs reached in a different way, but both have their gifts, and the pay is the prize. Jesus is the prize! God enters our life in different ways, so never expect it the exact same way as others, because we're different, and he knows how to lead you. The result will be the close relationship with your Savior and the individual experience it has in your life. Remember, only God will engineer experiences in your life to draw you to him, and he'll do that until your last breath because he loves you so much.

He'll never force it. It's always your choice to get that job and share the prize or live in this world wanting and not getting. Always an if, never a demand.

The challenge is not to see how good you can be. The challenge is how close you can get to Jesus and your Father on a personal level. That's true success in life. A relationship so close that you could feel his presence, his love, and his hurts, knowing without a doubt, no matter what this world throws, he'll always have your back. If you want that serenity, then go after it and *believe*! And he'll show you. It's that simple.

What Is My Purpose and What Is God's Will for My Life?

There is only one will of God and purpose on this earth, and that is to be one with the Father as Jesus is. When the Lord was here with us, he preached and healed the lost with many miracles and taught us how to pray, but the only prayers he ever did for us was asking his father to forgive us for such a horrible death on the cross and to *be one with him as he is*! This is God's will for your life, nothing else! That's the success we all long for, because he does everything through us, and we reap the rewards. People don't realize how God gets the glory. It means he wants you to be one with him, and the glory that comes through you is the Father. That peace and love comes from God in you, and you benefit from it. He made us in his image and likeness, meaning, we are to live as he lives—in the spirit forever. That's real life and what we were created for—total fulfillment, which is being blinded from the flesh.

We're trapped in a dead life, a life apart from him that we weren't created for. When he lives through you, you're feeling the life you were made to live (that beautiful diamond in the rough). It's like having a car, and only gas will make it go. If you fill it with anything else, it'll putter and putter trying to do what it was created for. Fill it with premium gas and it'll run smoothly as it should. No more choking, trying to make its way. The life we were made for has been stolen from us through sin, and God wants to make it right and give it back, our real life that was taken away. That's why we live with suffering and death, because of sin! God hates sin and destroyed it on the cross, and Satan knows it. There are real answers. You just need to listen and believe. God is real, always waiting and wanting to give you the peace that we long for and the tremendous joy that comes.

What are we really searching for?

If you ask anyone this one simple question, "What warms your heart?" The answer would be love. Being loved and accepted and giving the same. In the beginning of life, you search to surround yourself with people who like you, called friends, and the reason is because you want to be loved and accepted for who you are. It feels good. You fit in, and that's what makes you happy, having people who want to share time, and it feels great. Those who don't have this are very lonely and usually depressed. The saying (if you have one true friend, you are truly blessed), why is that so true? The fact is we were made for that purpose: to love and be loved.

Now let's look at people who do terrible things in life—lying, stealing, taking drugs, etc. Why do they do this? Is it because they surrounded themselves around people who accepted them? Made them feel like they were loved, even if it was wrong? Here is an example of what most people will do to fit in on a smaller scale. When you started to smoke cigarettes, you knew it was bad, and don't tell me you didn't! After coughing and your body telling you it wasn't good, you still did it. Why? *To fit in and be accepted.* Whether your friends are doing things that are good or bad, it doesn't matter because you long to be loved and accepted for who you are. That's the essence of life. You were created to be loved and to give love for eternity by God and your family, which you will have in heaven forever. The next time you see others doing evil, try to understand that they all long to be loved and accepted and guided to do the right things in life.

CHAPTER 15

The Beginning of the Truth

Did you ever think of how this all started? Back when Jesus was with us, it was expected from the believers that one day the Messiah would come back and destroy the people oppressing them. They thought revenge would be God's and he would eliminate the evil and gather them unto him as the true King to reign for eternity, but what they didn't know was how and when. Never realizing how much love and compassion our Lord has for all his creation, whether good or bad. His true message of peace and salvation wasn't through the way they thought. It was coming in love from within. The first to know the truth were the twelve apostles, disciples of the living God. When God's spirit came to live inside these first few, it revealed the message that no other soul had, and it was there mission to proclaim it to the rest of the world. Can you imagine? If you had friends and only you and them had the divine knowledge of what creation was all about (what the world was looking for all their lives), what would you do? When they received the Holy Spirit, they knew their lives would never be the same. The way they lived would change forever. The flesh was dead and the spirit of God controlled it. Salvation could only be done through the death and sacrifice of our Messiah. People must change within to have the love and peace we strive to get, and it could only be done with the power of the Holy Spirit. We can never do this with our own natural flesh, and God knew that. That's why he died so he can send his spirit to lift the blindness, the scales that covered our eyes. Can you imagine being the first to know this? Their mission was to go out and tell the rest of the world. Wow! It's been spreading ever since and will continue to do so until every soul has the opportunity to know the truth. Remember the story of the cave? You'll have a relationship with your Savior and can't wait to see him face-to-face. Why? Because you already know him. Experiencing a relationship from your Creator who acknowledges you as his child can't be put into words.

The Manual for Life

When you purchase a car, it comes with a manual. Why? To show you how the car functions, so if a problem appears, it will instruct you how to fix it. The manufacturer who created that car is the only one who can fix it. It knows all the parts and how it functions together to make it work. It's just like assembling a piece of furniture or a large toy with many parts. Without the instructions, you're lost. You have no idea even where to start. We try to avoid putting together something so complicated. Am I right? Who likes to try to put something together like this with no manual? Not me! Our life is the same. Everyone tries to figure out all the different parts of their life. What do we do to make us happy? Why are we here? Is there a God? Is there an afterlife? Should I be doing something different? Questions.

I'm not proud of some of the things I've done in my life. As we grow, all we're concerned with is having a good time, trying to fit in with others, seeking what we can get out of life for ourselves but never realizing who it may hurt along the way. We're so consumed about us that at times we are blind to the fact of how it affects others. Total ignorance. When God came in my life, everything changed! I couldn't believe what I surrounded my life with. He showed me what I was really missing and guided me to the manual for life, the holy written word of Almighty God—the Bible! It will show you how to fix your life so it runs smoothly, just like that car; the answers you've been looking for; the parts of the toy to assemble it correctly. So stop trying to figure it out and let the directions of the manual show you the way. It'll make your life so much easier because you'll understand how simple life can be.

What Is Leadership?

Jesus taught us that the least among you will be the greatest. When he walked with us and washed the feet of the apostles, he gave us an example of what we should do with our fellow man—serve! Leadership is nothing more than serving others. By doing this, you're leading others to follow. Putting yourself above others is not. Being a doormat is the calling of God. The apostles asked Jesus if they could sit at his side at the center of the great feast, in the end not realizing what they were saying, and Jesus once again said, "The least among you will be the first." Just by asking to be put in front of others show they only wanted to be the first. But again, the last will be! The humble and meek putting others ahead, these will be the first because they don't care to be recognized in any way. But God knows, and Jesus was our example. He is the Son of Almighty God who created the world and everything that exists. He came down to this darkened place and emptied himself of all glory to be a servant of the people, a doormat, mocked and tortured by the very creation he made. If this isn't the ultimate humiliation, then nothing is! He did this to show what true love is. Eternity with him isn't selfish or wanting, but giving, and the great reward is having that for eternity with the one who gave all for you—love, peace, and joy for all times. What an eternal life! Wow!

CHAPTER 16

Who Is God?

The only one that exists or that ever existed is God. And apart from him is nonexistence and is dark and void.

God created a form of existence to be with him, us! And apart from him who is existence, we are nonexistent, therefore dark and void.

God is Life. Life is existence, which is God. Apart from life, apart from God is death, which is nonexistence, therefore null and void. Death isn't created. It is the end result of not accepting existence.

God is Light. Light is existence. Apart from light there is no existence. Therefore, darkness is nonexistent and null and void. Darkness is not created. It is the end result of nonexistence.

God is Love. Love is existence. Apart from love there is no existence; therefore, hate is nonexistent and null and void. Hate not created. It is the end result of nonexistence

God is Goodness. Goodness is existence. Apart from goodness there is no existence; therefore, evil is nonexistent and null and void. Evil not created. It is the end result of nonexistence.

So all the end results, which are evil, hatred, and death, are void and actually created by us, not God. It is the result of (not accepting existence), who is God with life, love, light, and goodness.

The way to existence forever with God is life through Jesus, who is the Way, the truth, and the life. Without Jesus, who is life, you will be nonexistent, which is the result of total darkness, with hatred and lust for love, evil for good. God is the only one that exists. God is life, and without him, you will be the end result of what was created by you. Not of his creation, but yours!

Choices!

If you choose not to go to work, you get fired.

If you choose to go too close to a fire, you get burned.

If you choose not to want God, who is life and existence, then you won't.

Always a result from your free choices.

Before my relationship to God, I was the guy that was going to set the world on fire. My attitude was to go and live a life of luxury and ease. Believe me, I was sure putting the time in. I thought, *If a person didn't live well in life, then they were just lazy!* Don't get me wrong; there are those that do live off others and are lazy, but I'm not referring to them. If I can achieve being a millionaire, then anyone could, actually looking down on people who didn't have an abundance. I saw the power of money and wanted it, and I thank God daily for saving me from that life. He opened my eyes and humbled me and gave a glimpse of what would have been. I see what real joy is and the disaster I was heading for.

True happiness is nothing more than giving and helping your fellow man, not what you can gain in this world but what you can do to help others. I'm not saying you can't be wealthy and have joy in your life, but use the gifts God gave you to help others. Many people suffer through real circumstances. Even those who are doing well can collapse in a blink of an eye, through no fault of their own, and I thank him for showing me through my circumstances. He took my life and changed it to show what real people go through and how the power of money can so easily make you think a certain way.

In the Bible there's a story about a very rich man who came to Jesus and asked him what he has to do to enter the kingdom of heaven. Jesus replied, "Go sell everything that you have and come follow me." He knew exactly what he was saying, but he couldn't give up what he had here to get riches in heaven. The power of his money was too strong to let go. Then Jesus said these words: "It's harder for a camel to go through an eye of a needle than for a rich man to enter the kingdom of heaven." People interpret that wrong. What the true words mean in the language Jesus spoke is this: the eye of the needle simply means a doorway that isn't opened all the way. A tight squeeze. So if a camel would try to go through, it would be very difficult, not impossible. Having a lot of money entices the flesh to want more, and it makes it very hard to give it up to help others. We aren't here to help people who can help themselves. We're here to help those help themselves, to accomplish what they can do with the gifts God gave them. Real wealth is from within. The joy and peace we strive for is the counterfeit of what it truly is.

The whole truth is in these very words:

It's not who you *know*!

It's *who* you know.

That comfort and joy can only come from your Creator. He made you and knows exactly what your needs are. People have always asked the question, "What do you call success?" And the real answer is my personal relationship with *Jesus*. That's real wealth.

I challenge anyone who is listening to this message of love. If your heart is being tugged, and you hear the knocking at the door from your wonderful Father who created and loves you like no other, *open that door*! Let him come into your life. He tells us those who are called hear his voice. If you only realize your Father gave you a way. He *allowed* his Son to die a horrible death out of pure love, and by accepting that wonderful gift, you'll know the answers you've been looking for. Please don't wait till your last breath to meet him. It may be too late. By knowing him now is unbelievable, and the anticipation of seeing his face when you leave this world can't be put in words.

(Just repeat these words and allow God to enter in your life and reveal himself as he did with me. You will know your life is changing as the spirit starts to open your eyes to see the truth and love of God, who is your true father)

Dear lord, I know I'm a sinner and need your help to change. I believe that your son Jesus died on the cross for my sins and accept his suffering and death for my eternal salvation. Please forgive me and send

your Holy Spirit in my life to show me the way. I ask this in the wonderful name of your son and my savior Jesus Christ. Amen
Watch God Work!

ABOUT THE AUTHOR

P hilip Colagrande is one from a family of nine. He is married and blessed to a beautiful and faithful wife with three wonderful children. (Gifts of God) His life was drastically transformed by the call of God at the age of thirty and has never been the same since. Before his calling, he was going to set the world on fire, to become a very wealthy and successful man, all he can out of life. With all the long hours he put in to accomplish this, it just never worked out. This book is a testimony of how God's love worked through all his struggles. What he revealed to him is how simple life can be and how hard we make it! The true hidden life God has compelled him to share. True success he learned about life is not who you know; it's *who* you know.

CPSIA information can be obtained
at www.ICGtesting.com
Printed in the USA
LVHW020413170322
713568LV00007B/846